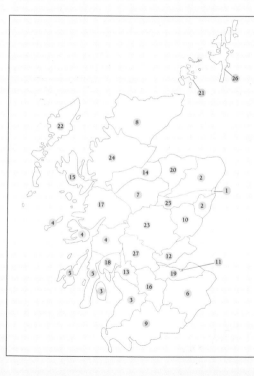

1. Abe...
2. Aberdeenshire
3. Arran & Ayrshire
4. Northern Argyll
5. Southern Argyll
6. The Borders
7. The Cairngorms
8. Caithness & Sutherland
9. Dumfries and Galloway
10. Dundee & Angus
11. Edinburgh
12. Fife, Kinross & Clackmannan
13. Glasgow
14. Inverness
18. Loch ... wal & Bute
19. The Lothians
20. Moray
21. Orkney
22. The Outer Hebrides
23. Perthshire
24. Ross & Cromarty
25. Royal Deeside
26. Shetland
27. Stirling & The Trossachs

The remaining two books, Distinguished Distilleries and Scotland's Mountains, feature locations throughout the country so are not included in the above list.

PICTURING SCOTLAND

LANARKSHIRE

NESS PUBLISHING

2 The beginning of Clydesdale at Watermeetings in the extreme south of Lanarkshire. As the name implies, this is where the confluence of Daer Water and Potrail Water gives birth to the River Clyde.

LANARKSHIRE

Welcome to Lanarkshire!

A TV advertisement for Scotland suggests that Scotland might surprise you. While that's true, it is also an understatement, as Scotland will frequently astonish you! The cause of that astonishment often arises when Scotland throws you something unexpected. This is Lanarkshire's trump card: for it is the only part of Scotland that has *two* World Heritage sites, namely New Lanark and the Antonine Wall (shared with neighbouring Falkirk). These two sites are therefore quite thoroughly illustrated in this book, but by no means do they monopolise the scenic delights of the area. Another winning card about Lanarkshire is the huge variety of terrain it encompasses, from its share of the Southern Uplands through the rolling agricultural landscape of Clydesdale, to urban images in the north.

Historically, Lanarkshire was the most populous county in Scotland but in those earlier times it was also considerably larger, incorporating Renfrewshire and Glasgow. Periodic re-organisations of local government, culminating in that of 1996, mean that the old area of Lanarkshire is now mainly occupied by the Unitary Authorities of North Lanarkshire and South Lanarkshire. The boundary between them reflects their differing characters. Broadly speaking, North Lanarkshire is the industrial part and South Lanarkshire the rural part. For convenience, this book will refer simply to 'Lanarkshire', except when more explicit definition is required. The story of Lanarkshire also embraces the story of the River Clyde. One of Scotland's great waterways,

Detail of Roman stonework in the bath-house at Bar Hill Fort on the Antonine Wall in North Lanarkshire, one of Lanarkshire's two World Heritage sites. See also pages 83-85.

it rises in the southern tip of the county and most of its 106-mile length lies within it (the last few miles, of course, flow through Glasgow). It will therefore be a recurring subject in the following pages.

The town of Lanark, located in the beautiful lower Clyde Valley, has had its share of significant events in the history of Scotland. In 978, it was the location of the first meeting of the Scots Parliament. It has been an important market town since medieval times, being granted the status of Royal Burgh by King David I in 1140. Its first church was founded in 630 and a Grammar School established in 1183. Of particular, if gruesome, note is that in 1297 William Wallace's wife was killed by the (English) sheriff of Lanark for refusing to divulge his hiding place. In reprisal, Wallace killed the sheriff and, in effect, sparked off the Scottish Wars of Independence. Today, it remains a bustling market town with a population of over 16,000 and is home to one of the busiest agricultural markets in Scotland.

New Lanark's World Heritage status owes as much to the ideas that were born there as the physical

6   Statue of James Douglas on the Cameronians' Regimental Memorial in Douglas, South Lanarkshire (see also pages 30-31).

aspects of the place and the story of regeneration that it represents. The enlightened management of founder David Dale's son-in-law Robert Owen transformed life in New Lanark with ideas and practices which were at least a hundred years ahead of their time. Child labour and corporal punishment were abolished and villagers were provided with decent homes, schools, evening classes, free health care and affordable food. He believed strongly in the importance of the environment and natural history and argued that a pleasant environment was essential for happy, healthy communities:

'They will be surrounded by gardens, have abundance of space in all directions to keep the air healthy and pleasant: they will have walks and plantations before them, and well cultivated grounds, kept in good order, as far as the eye can reach.'
(Robert Owen, 1817)

Part of the New Lanark Mills complex founded by David Dale in 1785, Lanarkshire's other World Heritage site (see also pages 36-46).

8   The southernmost part of Lanarkshire is neighboured by Dumfries & Galloway and Borders.
    Its scenery is a match for both those counties as this view demonstrates: just south of the village

of Coulter, this lovely dale typifies the landscape hereabouts. Livestock farming and forestry are the two principal types of land use. The Borders hills rise in the background.

10 The Leadhills and Wanlockhead narrow-gauge railway is high in the hills of south-western Lanarkshire and is built on the track-bed of the former standard-gauge line that served the lead mines.

The growing River Clyde is part of an evocative scene near the village of Crawford, next to a stand of **11** Scots Pine trees casting long shadows on the ground.

12 A couple of miles downstream, the castle in the village of Abington is long gone but would have looked like this model which is exhibited at Moat Park Heritage Centre in nearby Biggar (see p.27).

North of Abington and in the grip of winter, the Clyde continues its 106-mile journey to the sea. 13
The name Clyde comes from the Celtic 'clwyd' meaning strong, perhaps indicative of its current.

14 Looking across Clydesdale from Wandel towards Roberton, wintry conditions again create an atmospheric scene with Dungavel Hill partly visible beyond the village.

Lanarkshire's southern hills hide several reservoirs such as Coulter Reservoir at the head of Culter Water (note curious inconsistency about the spelling!). Mellow autumn tones surround the water. **15**

16 The view north down Culter (however it's spelled, it's pronounced 'Cooter') Dale looks towards, and across, Clydesdale. The most distant hills are those of Biggar Common.

This is the highest terrain in Lanarkshire, reaching 748m/2453ft at the summit of Culter Fell (above), **17** on the boundary with Borders. From the shoulder of hillside to its right comes the next picture . . .

18 . . . from Fell Shin. Clearly first-class walking country: looking north-west, in the foreground is Culter Dale, then Knowe Dod, Turkey Hill and Lamington Hill with Tinto Hill in the distance.

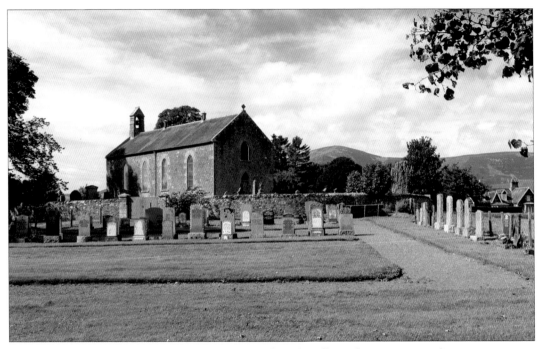

Returning to Clydesdale, this is St Ninian's Church in the village of Lamington. Built in 1721 over **19** the original Norman church, it incorporates a Romanesque doorway from the 1100s.

20 Glimpsed earlier (p.18), now we see Tinto Hill in all its considerable glory. Although not the highest at 707m/2319ft, it is Lanarkshire's most prominent and impressive hill, especially from the east.

Heading north-west, we come to the historic village of Coulter where this handsome period house **21** and its grounds create a perfect autumn vista.

22 Just a couple of miles on from Coulter is the attractive and historic town of Biggar. Its charms include this small burn (stream) and the garden around the War Memorial.

But today its particular claim to fame is the number of fascinating museums it possesses (six in all). **23**
This is Gladstone Court which recreates many shops and other businesses from times past.

24 Leaving Biggar briefly, this panorama a few miles from the town sums up the rural, agricultural nature of the area. South Lanarkshire is much more rural than North Lanarkshire and is almost four

times larger, with a population density of only 170 per sq. km. compared to 674 per sq. km. in N. Lanarkshire. The hills in the background are those explored on pages 15-18.

26 Returning to Biggar's museums, clockwise from top left: the toy shop window at Gladstone Court; the retort room at Biggar Gasworks Museum; a vintage Albion bus at the Albion Museum.

Moat Park Heritage Centre, Biggar, houses an eclectic range of displays such as the geology of the **27** area, life in the Iron Age, Roman invasion and models of local structures (as seen on p.12).

28 Biggar Kirk has a look of timeless solidity on its elevated position just to the north of the town centre. It dates to 1546, but there has been a church on this site for possibly as much as 1,500 years.

The village of Thankerton is a few miles west of Biggar and enjoys this view of the Clyde and the **29** surrounding landscape. From here we make a westerly detour to take in Douglas.

30 The village is named after the Black Douglas family, whose castle stood in this parkland. The ruin is all that remains of a larger construction, most of which was demolished due to mining subsidence.

In the village itself, the remnant of St Bride's Church is the oldest structure – a picturesque ruin. **31**
But its clock still functions and may be the oldest working clock in Scotland.

32 Returning to Clydesdale, this land is part of the Carmichael Estate, HQ of Clan Carmichael. Visitors can view the waxworks, go on one of the Estate's History Walks, then sample the tearoom!

Travelling north-west from Carmichael involves crossing the Clyde at Hyndford Bridge, from where **33** this beautiful winter landscape was recorded. Our next stop is the town of Lanark.

34 As befits the (former) county town, Lanark boasts some fine buildings. Left: St Nicholas Parish Church was built in 1774. Right: the Tolbooth on the High Street dates from 1778.

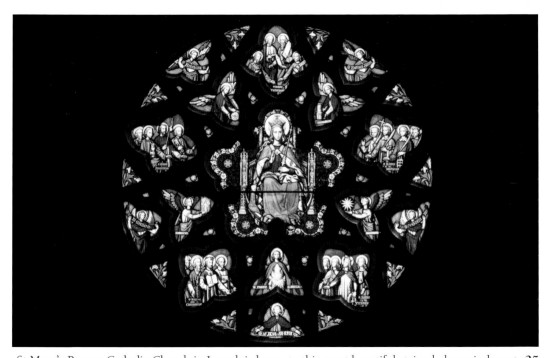

St Mary's Roman Catholic Church in Lanark is home to this most beautiful stained-glass window at **35** its east end above the altar. Opened in 1859, St Mary's was rebuilt in 1907 following a fire.

36 Following our first glimpse of New Lanark back on p.7, now it's time for a more thorough look. It grew from a mill into a model industrial community under the enlightened management of

David Dale's son-in-law Robert Owen from 1800–1825. As this picture shows, it is set deep in the **37** valley where it could exploit the power of the Clyde to drive the mill's machinery.

38 The river's power can reach awesome proportions in times of spate. Britain's first commercial hydro-electric power station was constructed just up-river from here in 1926 and is still in use today.

This is Mill Three which today houses preserved cotton mill machinery which is still in working **39** order, allowing visitors to see the plant in action. The mill lade flows past the building.

A mile or so upstream from New Lanark are the majestic Corra Linn falls. This 27m/90ft waterfall was immortalised in poetry by Wordsworth as 'the Clyde's most majestic daughter'. The Falls of Clyde are also a Scottish Wildlife Trust nature reserve where badgers, bats and peregrine falcons are among the resident creatures to be observed. The Trust runs a visitor centre at New Lanark and offers nature walks throughout the year.

42 New Lanark grew into a self-contained village that catered for all needs. Taken from outside David Dale's house, this picture looks towards the tenement row called New Building.

An important aspect of the enlightened approach to millworkers' education was the provision of the **43** Institute for the Formation of Character, pictured here, which is now the Visitor Centre.

44 This garden is at the heart of New Lanark, with Robert Owen's House in the centre of the picture, David Dale's house beyond and the village hall (formerly the church) on the hillside to the right.

Many interiors have been faithfully restored at New Lanark. This one re-creates a worker's cottage as **45** it would have been in the 1930s. A bedroom can be seen leading off the living room.

46 The village store was located in the main millworkers' housing block and pioneered the ideas on which the Co-operative movement was later founded.

A complete change of scene now, as the Clyde shows off another of its moods at sunrise near the **47** village of Carstairs, a few miles from Lanark.

48 The Clyde Valley around Lanark is flanked by rich farmland, with a higher proportion of arable than we have seen so far. Perhaps there is a reason for the curious kinks in the wheel tracks going through

the grain fields! These two pictures were taken from Blackhill, west of Lanark. The one above looks south, made all the more attractive by the mix of trees among the fields. **49**

50 Standing above the River Nethan (a tributary of the Clyde), Craignethan Castle is an exceptional fortress-residence. Here, the main tower is viewed across the outer and inner courtyards.

Built around 1530, it was the brainchild of Sir James Hamilton of Finnart, King James V's master of works. Above: east elevation of the main tower with remains of the east range in the foreground.

51

52 Continuing north along the course of the Clyde, this bridge at Rosebank is typical of the sturdy yet elegant structures that span the river.

Just down-river from Rosebank is the hamlet of Dalserf where this unusual but handsome church **53** was built in 1655 for a Covenanter (Presbyterian rather than Episcopalian) congregation.

54 Now another westerly hop to reach the picturesque town of Strathaven. The town holds an annual hot air balloon festival, the only one of its kind in Scotland and one of the largest in the UK.

In a town blessed with so much to see, the finest sight of all is the centrepiece of Allison Green with **55** Powmillon Burn flowing through and East Parish Church at the far end.

56 Just south of Hamilton, Chatelherault was designed by the famous Scottish architect William Adam and built in 1732 as the hunting lodge and summer house for the wealthy Duke of Hamilton.

The restored building is now a visitor centre with exhibitions on the area's history, wildlife and the story of Chatelherault itself. The Duke's private Banqueting Room and apartments are open to visitors.

58 And so to Hamilton itself, a large town with a wealth of mostly industrial-era architecture. Most impressive is Hamilton Townhouse, built in three stages from 1907 to 1928.

Left: the remarkable 37m/123ft tall Hamilton Mausoleum was begun in 1842 for the 10th Duke. **59**
Right: one of several intriguing sculptures in the park between Back Row and Cadzow Burn, Hamilton.

60 Blantyre lies to the north of Hamilton and is the birthplace of David Livingstone, Scotland's most famous explorer and missionary. The Livingstones shared this tenement, Shuttle Row, with 23 other

families. David was born in this room in 1813. This historic attraction is packed with items relating **61** to his explorations in Africa, including a statue of him being attacked by a lion (see p.96). A cast of

62 his arm bone shows the fractures inflicted by the attack. He died in Africa and, here in the chapel, the carving on the left depicts his body being carried to its resting place.

A few miles to the west, on the outskirts of the new town of East Kilbride, is the Museum of Rural 63
Life. In a well-balanced blend of displays like the one above and a working farm set in the 1950s,

64 set in the 1950s, it presents fascinating insights into Lanarkshire's rural past. Left: an example of the farm's livestock. Right: the Clydesdale horse is also an important part of Scotland's working past.

This aerial view introduces North Lanarkshire and shows the locations on the next few pages. **65**
The Clyde is at the bottom of the picture; note the castle and the loch at top right.

66 Again from the air, the overall plan and strategic location of Bothwell Castle can be appreciated. The substantial remains of the keep are at the right of the picture. This is Scotland's largest and

finest 13th century castle. Not surprisingly, it figured prominently in the Wars of Independence with England. Siege followed on siege. The most momentous was Edward I's great siege of 1301.

68 In the village of Bothwell the Parish Church is locally known as the 'Cathedral of Lanarkshire'.
Right: memorial to the poet Joanna Baillie, born in Bothwell Manse in 1762; she died in London in 1851.

Strathclyde Country Park sits between Hamilton and Motherwell. The focus of the park is this loch **69** (seen in the picture on p.65) around which is a network of loch-side and woodland paths for walking

70 and cycling. As this picture shows, water sports are a major theme, with sailing, kayaking, rowing and speed-boat rides all available. Scotland's Theme Park is located at the northern end of the loch.

The viewing tower at Motherwell Heritage Centre provides great views over the town, aided on this occasion by a moment of dramatic light. Inset: detail of period display in the Centre.

72 A little to the north in the town of Coatbridge is Summerlee – the Museum of Scottish Industrial Life. Set in 22 acres, it is based around the site of the 19th century Summerlee Ironworks.

This is the view that greets visitors as they enter – a sight guaranteed to quicken the pulse of all those with any interest in industrial heritage, and which will capture the imagination of the rest!

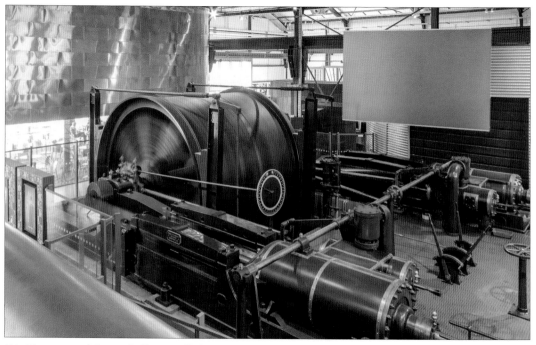

74 The main exhibition hall is an Alladin's Cave of engineering prowess, including this stationary colliery steam winding engine, today powered electrically so its motion can still be appreciated.

Among the many exhibits outside, these silhouetted cranes look rather like huge mechanical **75** dinosaurs. Thanks to Summerlee, by the 1850s, Coatbridge had become known as the 'Iron Burgh'.

76 Summerlee is home to Scotland's only operational heritage tramway. Here, one of the trams trundles another group of visitors past the re-created mine which can also be explored.

Left: the mine's winding gear, seen through an elaborate Victorian iron structure that would 77 probably have housed a drinking fountain. Right: period advertisement c.1900.

78 Several miners' cottages have been restored to represent different eras from 1840 (seen here) to 1980. If Summerlee is to be experienced and enjoyed to the full, make sure you allow a whole day there.

The new town of Cumbernauld may have its detractors, but credit should be given to creative attempts to add character and colour here and there, such as in the residential district of Condorrat.

80 Palacerigg Country Park is set in the hills to the south-east of Cumbernauld. It features a zoo, among the residents of which are this rare-breed cow, goats and delightful crested ducks.

Nature trails wind their way around the 40-hectare site from which deer, badgers, foxes, hares and **81** various birds of prey may be seen . . . Inset: . . . and peacocks!

82 Just north of Cumbernauld is the beautiful Kelvin valley, tantalising glimpses of which appear
through the trees on Bar Hill, close to the village of Twechar. The Antonine Wall, built by the Romans

from AD142 to 144, runs through here. Bar Hill is the highest fort on the Wall, containing the foundations of the headquarters building and a bath-house. Remains of the latter are pictured here.

84 Left: another piece of bath-house detail. Right: a little further east, this sign directs the way to the next section of the Antonine Wall, on Croy Hill.

Up on Croy Hill, this is perhaps the best site to appreciate the strategic significance of the Antonine **85** Wall and enjoy the superb views over the Kelvin Valley. The Wall's ditch is in the foreground.

86 The vantage point of Croy Hill reveals much more of interest such as our next destinations of Auchinstarry Marina and Auchinstarry Quarry, indicated by the crags to the upper right.

Boats, on a still, bright autumn morning, always appeal. Auchinstarry Marina is on the Forth & **87** Clyde Canal that was built from 1768 to 1790 to connect the North Sea with the Firth of Clyde.

88 A brief return now to Croy Hill to enjoy this Kelvin valley panorama. The Antonine Wall comes over the hills on the left from Bar Hill Fort through the nick in the trees on the skyline, then passes

through the middle of the foreground. The distant lands at top right are in neighbouring East Dunbartonshire, with the Campsie Fells on the horizon.

90 The disused quarry at Auchinstarry, just outside the town of Kilsyth, has become a great recreational amenity, and not just for enabling lovely reflection shots like this.

Over time the disused workings have filled with water to form Auchinstarry Loch. Now stocked with a variety of fish it is a favourite spot for local anglers.

92 Rather more dramatically, it has become a magnet for rock climbers, the dolerite cliffs being divided into various routes with emotive name like 'Scream', 'Slinky Lizard' and 'Death is the Hunter'!

On the eastern edge of Kilsyth is Colzium Lennox Estate, centred on this mansion house. It was **93** built in 1783, enlarged in 1861, and today houses a museum with displays relating to local heritage.

94 Behind the house is a fine walled garden stocked with an interesting variety of shrubs and trees. Elsewhere on the estate are the remains of a tower house and a restored ice-house.

And this is journey's end, a last look across the Kelvin Valley to the backdrop of the Kilsyth Hills. **95**
To the north they drop down to Carron Valley and Stirlingshire, but that's another tour . . .

Published 2014 by Ness Publishing, 47 Academy Street, Elgin, Moray, IV30 1LR
Phone/fax 01343 549663   www.nesspublishing.co.uk

All photographs © Colin and Eithne Nutt except pp.2-3, 11, 18, 33, 47, 52 & 53 © Keith Fergus;
p.54 © Gordon McAllan; p.64 (right) © Jacqueline Pettigrew, *The Scottish Farmer*; 65 & 66 © Guthrie Aerial Photography

Text © Colin Nutt
ISBN 978-1-906549-25-1

Front cover: at New Lanark; p.1: swan at Auchinstarry Marina; p.4: Clydesdale Heavy Horse; this page: David Livingstone and lion statue, Blantyre; back cover: sunset at Baron's Haugh Nature Reserve, Motherwell

For a list of websites and phone numbers please turn over > > > >

Websites and phone numbers (where available) of featured places in alphabetical order:

Albion Museum, Biggar: www.albion-trust.org.uk (T) 01899 221497
Auchinstarry Quarry (re. climbing): www.scottishclimbs.com
Bar Hill Fort (Antonine Wall): www.historic-scotland.gov.uk
Biggar Gasworks Museum: www.historic-scotland.gov.uk (T) 01899 220070
Biggar Kirk: www.biggarkirk.btck.co.uk
Biggar Museums: www.biggarmuseumtrust.co.uk (T) 01899 221050
Bothwell Castle: www.historic-scotland.gov.uk (T) 01698 816894
Carmichael Farm Shop & Visitor Centre: www.carmichael.co.uk (T) 01899 308336
New Lanark: www.newlanark.org (T) 01555 661345
Chatelherault Country Park: www.visitlanarkshire.com (T) 01698 543402
Colzium House Museum: www.northlanarkshire.gov.uk (T) 01236 638352
Craignethan Castle: www.historic-scotland.gov.uk (T) 01555 860364
Dalserf Church: www.dalserf.org
David Livingstone Centre: www.nts.org.uk (T) 0844 493 2207
Douglas: www.douglashistory.co.uk
Falls of Clyde: scottishwildlifetrust.org.uk (T) 01555 665262
Forth & Clyde Canal: www.scottishcanals.co.uk
Hamilton Mausoleum: www.visitlanarkshire.com (T) 01698 328232
Lanark: www.lanark.co.uk and www.visitlanarkshire.com
Leadhills and Wanlockhead Railway: www.leadhillsrailway.co.uk
National Museum of Rural Life: www.nms.ac.uk (T) 0300 123 6789
Palacerigg Country Park: www.visitlanarkshire.com (T) 01236 720047
Summerlee Industrial Museum: www.northlanarkshire.gov.uk (T) 01236 638460